stars The World's greatest sports stars
stars The World's
The World's Greatest Sports Stars

Sports Illustrated KIDS

The World's Greatest
Basketball Players

by Matt Doeden

CAPSTONE PRESS
a capstone imprint

Sports Illustrated KIDS The World's Greatest Sports Stars is published by Capstone Press,
151 Good Counsel Drive, P.O. Box 669, Mankato, Minnesota 56002.
www.capstonepub.com

Books published by Capstone Press are manufactured with paper
containing at least 10 percent post-consumer waste.

Library of Congress Cataloging-in-Publication Data
Doeden, Matt.
    The world's greatest basketball players / by Matt Doeden.
    p. cm. — (Sports Illustrated KIDS. the world's greatest sports stars)
    Includes bibliographical references and index.
    Summary: "Describes the achievements and career statistics of basketball's greatest
stars" — Provided by publisher.
    ISBN 978-1-4296-3923-1 (library binding)
    ISBN 978-1-4296-4869-1 (paperback)
    1. Basketball players — Biography — Juvenile literature. 2. Basketball players —
Rating of — Juvenile literature. I. Title. II. Series.
GV884.A1D64 2010
796.323092'2 — dc22
[B]   2009028535

Editorial Credits
Aaron Sautter, editor; Tracy Davies, designer; Eric Gohl, media researcher;
    Laura Manthe, production specialist

Photo Credits
Shutterstock/Ksash, backgrounds
Sports Illustrated/Bill Frakes, 1 (left), 18; Bob Rosato, 1 (center), 11, 12, 28;
    Damian Strohmeyer, 6, 8; David E. Klutho, 17; John Biever, 5 (both), 25;
    John W. McDonough, cover, 1 (right), 4 (left), 15, 21, 22, 26; Manny Millan,
    4–5 (background), 4 (right), 30–31 (background)

Statistics in this book are current through the 2008–2009 NBA season.

Printed in the United States of America in Stevens Point, Wisconsin.
022011   006074R

Table of Contents

Game On!

Swish! Kobe Bryant sinks a long three-pointer. Thud! Tim Duncan blocks a shot before the ball goes in the net. Basketball is packed with action. Fans across the country love watching monster dunks and long-range bombs. The biggest stars of the National Basketball Association (NBA) bring loads of excitement to the court.

slam **dunks**   big-time **blocks**

amazing **shots**

intense **action**

Kobe Bryant

Kobe Bryant thrives in the clutch. The Los Angeles Lakers guard is at his best when the game is on the line. He can shoot from the outside or drive into the lane and score inside. Bryant is a great defender too. He's been selected to the NBA's All-Defensive First Team seven times. Bryant was the 2007–2008 NBA Most Valuable Player (MVP). He is also a four-time NBA champion.

Regular Season Stats

Year	Team	Games	PPG	RPG	APG	SPG
1996–1997	LAL	71	7.6	1.9	1.3	0.7
1997–1998	LAL	79	15.4	3.1	2.5	0.9
1998–1999	LAL	50	19.9	5.3	3.8	1.4
1999–2000	LAL	66	22.5	6.3	4.9	1.6
2000–2001	LAL	68	28.5	5.9	5.0	1.7
2001–2002	LAL	80	25.2	5.5	5.5	1.5
2002–2003	LAL	82	30.0	6.9	5.9	2.2
2003–2004	LAL	65	24.0	5.5	5.1	1.7
2004–2005	LAL	66	27.6	5.9	6.0	1.3
2005–2006	LAL	80	35.4	5.3	4.5	1.8
2006–2007	LAL	77	31.6	5.7	5.4	1.4
2007–2008	LAL	82	28.3	6.3	5.4	1.8
2008–2009	LAL	82	26.8	5.2	4.9	1.5
CAREER		**948**	**25.1**	**5.3**	**4.6**	**1.5**

(PPG = points per game; RPG = rebounds per game;
APG = assists per game; SPG = steals per game)

achievements

All-Star selection: 1998, 2000, 2001, 2002, 2003,
    2004, 2005, 2006, 2007, 2008, 2009
All-Star Game MVP: 2002, 2007, 2009
NBA MVP: 2007–2008
NBA Finals MVP: 2009
NBA All-Defensive First Team: 2000, 2003, 2004, 2006,
    2007, 2008, 2009
Averaged career-high 35.4 points per game in 2005-06

clutch: a crucial moment in a game when an important play must be made

fact

Bryant's father was Joe "Jellybean" Bryant.
He played for the Philadelphia 76ers, San
Diego Clippers, and Houston Rockets.

Kevin Garnett

Kevin Garnett can do almost anything on a basketball court. He can grab **rebounds**. He can score inside. And he has a soft shooting touch. He can also pass like a guard or defend almost any player. In 2004, "The Big Ticket" won the league MVP award with the Minnesota Timberwolves. In 2008, he led the Boston Celtics to an NBA championship.

Name: Kevin Maurice Garnett
Born: May 19, 1976, in Mauldin, South Carolina
Height: 6 feet, 11 inches
Weight: 253 pounds
Position: Forward

Regular Season Stats

Year	Team	Games	PPG	RPG	APG	BPG
1995–1996	MIN	80	10.4	6.3	1.8	1.6
1996–1997	MIN	77	17.0	8.0	3.1	2.1
1997–1998	MIN	82	18.5	9.6	4.2	1.8
1998–1999	MIN	47	20.8	10.4	4.3	1.8
1999–2000	MIN	81	22.9	11.8	5.0	1.6
2000–2001	MIN	81	22.0	11.4	5.0	1.8
2001–2002	MIN	81	21.2	12.1	5.2	1.6
2002–2003	MIN	82	23.0	13.4	6.0	1.6
2003–2004	MIN	82	24.2	13.9	5.0	2.2
2004–2005	MIN	82	22.2	13.5	5.7	1.4
2005–2006	MIN	76	21.8	12.7	4.1	1.4
2006–2007	MIN	76	22.4	12.8	4.1	1.7
2007–2008	BOS	71	18.8	9.2	3.4	1.3
2008–2009	BOS	57	15.8	8.5	2.5	1.2
CAREER		**1055**	**20.2**	**11.1**	**4.3**	**1.6**

(PPG = points per game; RPG = rebounds per game;
APG = assists per game; BPG= blocks per game)

achievements

All-Star selection: 1997, 1998, 2000, 2001, 2002,
2003, 2004, 2005, 2006, 2007, 2008, 2009
All-Star Game MVP: 2003
NBA MVP: 2004
NBA Defensive Player of the Year: 2008
NBA champion: 2008

rebound: to gain possession of the ball after someone attempts a shot at the basket

fact

Garnett averaged at least 20 points,
10 rebounds, and five assists per game
for a record six straight seasons.

Name: Dirk Nowitzki
Born: June 19, 1978, in Wurzburg, Germany
Height: 7 feet
Weight: 245 pounds
Position: Forward

Regular Season Stats

Year	Team	Games	PPG	RPG	APG	SPG
1998–1999	DAL	47	8.2	3.4	1.0	0.6
1999–2000	DAL	82	17.5	6.5	2.5	0.8
2000–2001	DAL	82	21.8	9.2	2.1	1.0
2001–2002	DAL	76	23.4	9.9	2.4	1.1
2002–2003	DAL	80	25.1	9.9	3.0	1.4
2003–2004	DAL	77	21.8	8.7	2.7	1.2
2004–2005	DAL	78	26.1	9.7	3.1	1.2
2005–2006	DAL	81	26.6	9.0	2.8	0.7
2006–2007	DAL	78	24.6	8.9	3.4	0.7
2007–2008	DAL	77	23.6	8.6	3.5	0.7
2008–2009	DAL	81	25.9	8.4	2.4	0.8
CAREER		**839**	**22.7**	**8.6**	**2.7**	**0.9**

(PPG= points per game; RPG = rebounds per game;
APG = assists per game; SPG = steals per game)

achievements

All-Star selection: 2003, 2004, 2005, 2006,
    2007, 2008, 2009
NBA MVP Award: 2007
All-NBA First Team: 2005, 2006, 2007
NBA Three-Point Shootout winner: 2006
Helped Germany's national team qualify for
    the 2008 Olympic Games

fact

Nowitzki had the honor of carrying
Germany's flag in the Opening Ceremonies
of the 2008 Olympic Games.

Dirk Nowitzki

Big men like Dirk Nowitzki don't usually have the skills of a shooting guard. But he handles and passes the ball with ease. And he's one of the best three-point shooters in the league. Nowitzki is also a great inside scorer and rebounder for the Dallas Mavericks. His great all-around play earned Nowitzki NBA MVP honors for the 2006–2007 season.

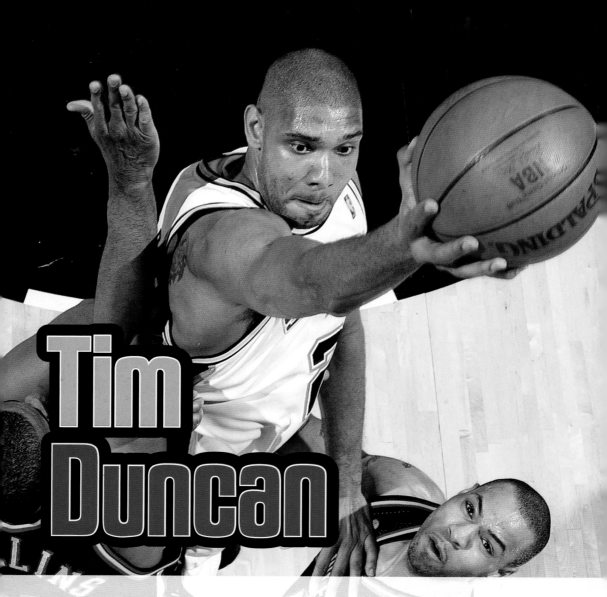

Tim Duncan

Tim Duncan isn't flashy, but he's a winner. The San Antonio Spurs forward rarely shows emotion on the court. But he's a real force in the **paint**. Duncan is a great rebounder and inside scorer. He's one of the league's best defenders too. Duncan's skills have helped him win two MVP awards and four NBA championships.

personal information

Name: Timothy Theodore Duncan
Born: April 25, 1976, in St. Croix,
    U.S. Virgin Islands
College: Wake Forest University
Height: 6 feet, 11 inches   Weight: 260 pounds
Position: Forward / Center

Regular Season Stats

Year	Team	Games	PPG	RPG	APG	BPG
1997–1998	SAS	82	21.1	11.9	2.7	2.5
1998–1999	SAS	50	21.7	11.4	2.4	2.5
1999–2000	SAS	74	23.2	12.4	3.2	2.2
2000–2001	SAS	82	22.2	12.2	3.0	2.3
2001–2002	SAS	82	25.5	12.7	3.7	2.5
2002–2003	SAS	81	23.3	12.9	3.9	2.9
2003–2004	SAS	69	22.3	12.4	3.1	2.7
2004–2005	SAS	66	20.3	11.1	2.7	2.6
2005–2006	SAS	80	18.6	11.0	3.2	2.0
2006–2007	SAS	80	20.0	10.6	3.4	2.4
2007–2008	SAS	78	19.3	11.3	2.8	1.9
2008–2009	SAS	75	19.3	10.7	3.5	1.7
CAREER		**899**	**21.4**	**11.7**	**3.2**	**2.4**

(PPG = points per game; RPG = rebounds per game;
APG = assists per game; BPG=blocks per game)

achievements

All-Star selection: 1998, 2000, 2001, 2002, 2003,
    2004, 2005, 2006, 2007, 2008, 2009
NBA MVP: 2002, 2003
Rookie of the Year: 1998
NBA Finals MVP: 1999, 2003, 2005
NBA champion: 1999, 2003, 2005, 2007

paint: the painted area directly below and in front of the basket

fact

Duncan grew up wanting to be a swimmer.
He switched to basketball after a hurricane
destroyed the only large pool near his home.

Name: Christopher Emmanuel Paul
Born: May 6, 1985, in Winston-Salem,
   North Carolina
College: Wake Forest University
Height: 6 feet   Weight: 175 pounds
Position: Guard

Regular Season Stats

Year	Team	Games	PPG	RPG	APG	SPG
2005–2006	NOR	78	16.1	5.1	7.8	2.2
2006–2007	NOR	64	17.3	4.4	8.9	1.8
2007–2008	NOR	80	21.1	4.0	11.6	2.7
2008–2009	NOR	78	22.8	5.5	11.0	2.8
CAREER		**300**	**19.4**	**4.8**	**9.9**	**2.4**

(PPG = points per game; RPG = rebounds per game;
APG = assists per game; SPG = steals per game)

achievements

All-Star selection: 2008, 2009
Rookie of the Year Award: 2006
NBA assists leader: 2008, 2009
All-NBA First Team: 2008, 2009
Member of U.S. Olympic gold medal team: 2008

fact | Paul set an NBA record by making at
least one steal in 108 straight games.

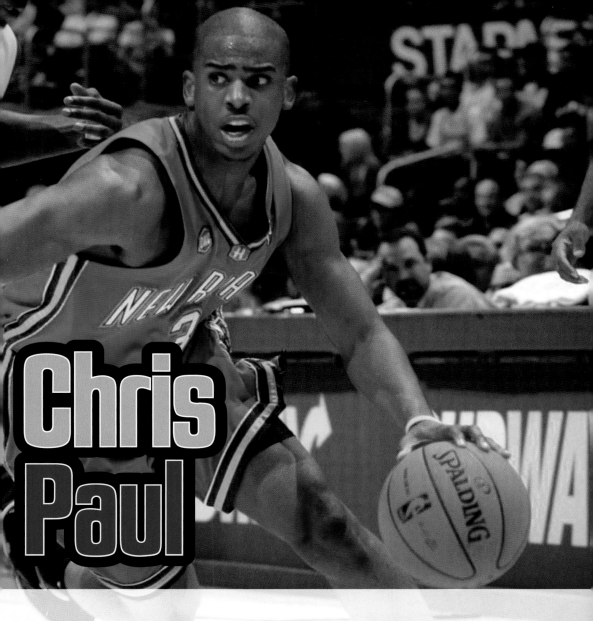

Chris Paul

Nobody drives into the paint or passes like the New Orleans Hornets' Chris Paul. If a shot is open, he'll take it. If not, he'll pass the ball to an open teammate. Paul's great passing makes him one of the league's best point guards. He led the NBA in assists in the 2007–2008 and 2008–2009 seasons.

personal information

Name: LeBron Raymone James
Born: December 30, 1984, in Akron, Ohio
Height: 6 feet, 8 inches
Weight: 250 pounds
Position: Forward

Regular Season Stats

Year	Team	Games	PPG	RPG	APG	SPG
2003–2004	CLE	79	20.9	5.5	5.9	1.6
2004–2005	CLE	80	27.2	7.4	7.2	2.2
2005–2006	CLE	79	31.4	7.0	6.6	1.6
2006–2007	CLE	78	27.3	6.7	6.0	1.6
2007–2008	CLE	75	30.0	7.9	7.2	1.8
2008–2009	CLE	81	28.4	7.6	7.2	1.7
CAREER		**472**	**27.5**	**7.0**	**6.7**	**1.8**

(PPG = points per game; RPG = rebounds per game;
APG = assists per game; SPG = steals per game)

achievements

All-Star selection: 2005, 2006, 2007,
    2008, 2009
All-Star Game MVP: 2006, 2008
NBA MVP: 2009
Rookie of the Year Award: 2004
All-NBA First Team: 2006, 2008, 2009
NBA scoring champion: 2008

fact James has played for the U.S. Olympic basketball team twice. In 2004, he and the U.S. team won the bronze medal. In 2008, they won gold.

LeBron James

Nobody's going to stop LeBron James when he wants to score. James has a rare combination of speed and strength. He's almost impossible to guard. James was a huge star even before he was a pro. In 2003, he went straight from high school to the Cleveland Cavaliers. His soft touch and powerful style helped him become the 2008–2009 NBA MVP.

Dwight Howard

Dwight Howard is a beast in the paint. Nobody works harder to block the ball and grab rebounds. The Orlando Magic made him the top pick of the 2004 NBA **Draft**. He is one of the NBA's best rebounders. Howard knows how to put up points too. Put it all together and he's possibly the best young "big man" in the NBA.

Name: Dwight David Howard
Born: December 8, 1985, in Atlanta, Georgia
Height: 6 feet, 11 inches
Weight: 240 pounds
Position: Center

Regular Season Stats

Year	Team	Games	PPG	RPG	APG	BPG
2004–2005	ORL	82	12.0	10.0	0.9	1.7
2005–2006	ORL	82	15.8	12.5	1.5	1.4
2006–2007	ORL	82	17.6	12.3	1.9	1.9
2007–2008	ORL	82	20.7	14.2	1.3	2.1
2008–2009	ORL	79	20.6	13.8	1.4	2.9
CAREER		**407**	**17.3**	**12.5**	**1.4**	**2.0**

(PPG = points per game; RPG = rebounds per game;
APG = assists per game; BPG = blocks per game)

achievements

All-Star selection: 2007, 2008, 2009
All-NBA First Team: 2008, 2009
Led NBA in total rebounds: 2006, 2007,
    2008, 2009
Youngest player in NBA history to reach
    5,000 career rebounds
Number-one overall pick of 2004 NBA Draft

draft: an event when an athlete is chosen to join a professional sports team

fact

Howard won the 2008 NBA All-Star Slam Dunk Contest. In one of his dunks, he wore a Superman cape. He took off from beyond the free-throw line to make a huge slam dunk.

Name: Yao Ming
Born: September 12, 1980, in Shanghai, China
Height: 7 feet, 6 inches
Weight: 310 pounds
Position: Center

Regular Season Stats

Year	Team	Games	PPG	RPG	APG	BPG
2002–2003	HOU	82	13.5	8.2	1.7	1.8
2003–2004	HOU	82	17.5	9.0	1.5	1.9
2004–2005	HOU	80	18.3	8.4	0.8	2.0
2005–2006	HOU	57	22.3	10.2	1.5	1.6
2006–2007	HOU	48	25.0	9.4	2.0	2.0
2007–2008	HOU	55	22.0	10.8	2.3	2.0
2008–2009	HOU	77	19.7	9.9	1.8	1.9
CAREER		**481**	**19.1**	**9.3**	**1.6**	**1.9**

(PPG = points per game; RPG = rebounds per game
APG = assists per game; BPG = blocks per game)

achievements

All-Star selection: 2003, 2004, 2005, 2006,
      2007, 2008, 2009
NBA All-Rookie Team: 2003
Top overall pick of the 2002 NBA Draft
Chinese Basketball Association MVP: 2001, 2002
Chinese Basketball Association champion: 2002

fact

Yao's mother played for the Chinese
women's national team. His father also
played for the Shanghai team in China.

Yao Ming

Yao Ming towers over his competitors. At 7½ feet tall, he is the NBA's tallest player. He's also an international superstar. Yao was only the second player from China to join the NBA. In his home country, he led the Shanghai Sharks to a league championship in 2002. Later that year, the Houston Rockets made him the first overall pick of the draft.

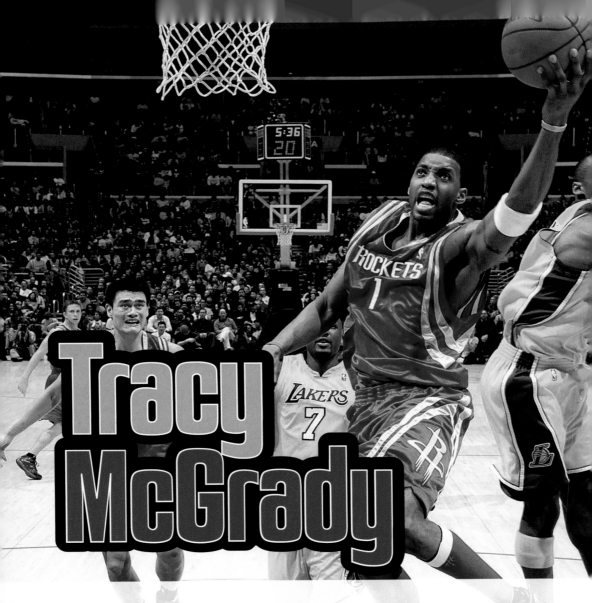

Tracy McGrady

Tracy McGrady can score from almost anywhere on the court. He can slash toward the hoop for a **layup**. Or he can step back and launch a long three-pointer. McGrady was the NBA's scoring champ twice while with the Orlando Magic. He was traded to the Houston Rockets in 2004. Since then, he has remained one of the game's best scorers.

Name: Tracy Lamar McGrady Jr.
Born: May 24, 1979, in Bartow, Florida
Height: 6 feet, 8 inches
Weight: 223 pounds
Position: Guard

Regular Season Stats

Year	Team	Games	PPG	RPG	APG	SPG
1997–1998	TOR	64	7.0	4.2	1.5	0.8
1998–1999	TOR	49	9.3	5.7	2.3	1.1
1999–2000	TOR	79	15.4	6.3	3.3	1.1
2000–2001	ORL	77	26.8	7.5	4.6	1.5
2001–2002	ORL	76	25.6	7.9	5.3	1.6
2002–2003	ORL	75	32.1	6.5	5.5	1.7
2003–2004	ORL	67	28.0	6.0	5.5	1.4
2004–2005	HOU	78	25.7	6.2	5.7	1.7
2005–2006	HOU	47	24.4	6.5	4.8	1.3
2006–2007	HOU	71	24.6	5.3	6.5	1.3
2007–2008	HOU	66	21.6	5.1	5.9	1.0
2008–2009	HOU	35	15.6	4.4	5.0	1.2
CAREER		**784**	**22.1**	**6.1**	**4.7**	**1.3**

(PPG = points per game; RPG = rebounds per game;
APG = assists per game; SPG = steals per game)

layup: a shot where the ball is gently played off the backboard and into the basket

achievements

All-Star selection: 2001, 2002, 2003, 2004,
 2005, 2006, 2007
NBA Most Improved Player Award: 2001
All-NBA First Team: 2002, 2003
NBA scoring champion: 2002, 2003
Made NBA record 8 three-pointers in one half
 on January 26, 2004

fact

McGrady and the Orlando Magic's Vince Carter are third cousins. They both played for the Toronto Raptors in the late 1990s.

Name: Paul Anthony Pierce
Born: October 13, 1977, in Oakland, California
College: University of Kansas
Height: 6 feet, 7 inches
Weight: 235 pounds
Position: Forward

Regular Season Stats

Year	Team	Games	PPG	RPG	APG	SPG
1998–1999	BOS	48	16.5	6.4	2.4	1.7
1999–2000	BOS	73	19.5	5.4	3.0	2.1
2000–2001	BOS	82	25.3	6.4	3.1	1.7
2001–2002	BOS	82	26.1	6.9	3.2	1.9
2002–2003	BOS	79	25.9	7.3	4.4	1.8
2003–2004	BOS	80	23.0	6.5	5.1	1.6
2004–2005	BOS	82	21.6	6.6	4.2	1.6
2005–2006	BOS	79	26.8	6.7	4.7	1.4
2006–2007	BOS	47	25.0	5.9	4.1	1.0
2007–2008	BOS	80	19.6	5.1	4.5	1.3
2008–2009	BOS	81	20.5	5.6	3.6	1.0
CAREER		**813**	**22.9**	**6.3**	**3.9**	**1.6**

(PPG = points per game; RPG = rebounds per game;
APG = assists per game; SPG = steals per game)

achievements

All-Star selection: 2002, 2003, 2004, 2005,
    2006, 2008, 2009
NBA Finals MVP: 2008
NBA champion: 2008
NBA All-Rookie First Team: 1999
NCAA First-Team All-America: 1998

fact | Pierce's nickname is "The Truth." It was
given to him by center Shaquille O'Neal.

Paul Pierce

In Game 1 of the 2008 NBA Finals, Boston's Paul Pierce injured his knee. But he shrugged off the pain and returned to the court. He led the Celtics to a victory. The team went on to win the NBA title. Pierce's sweet shooting and tough play made him the NBA Finals MVP that season.

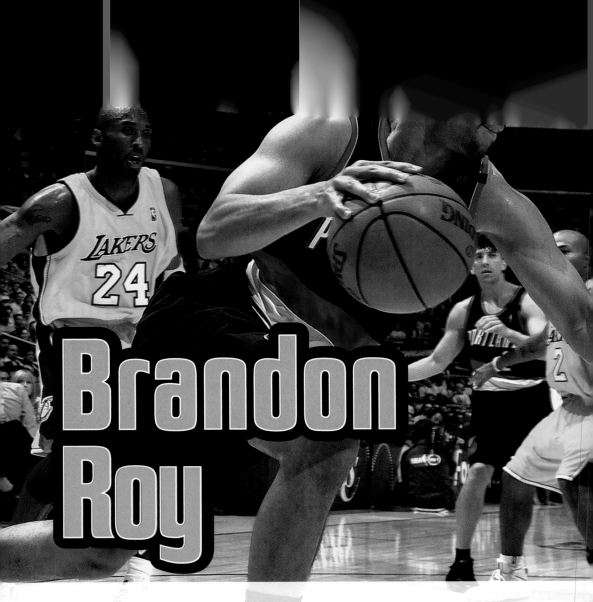

Brandon Roy

Brandon Roy quickly made his mark in the NBA. In 2006, he scored 20 points in his first game with the Portland Trail Blazers. Then he scored 19 in his second game. Roy's accurate shooting, passing ability, and good defense quickly made him a star. He won the **Rookie** of the Year award in 2007. By his second year, he was already an All-Star.

Name: Brandon Dawayne Roy
Born: July 23, 1984, in Seattle, Washington
College: University of Washington
Height: 6 feet, 6 inches
Weight: 211 pounds
Position: Guard

Regular Season Stats

Year	Team	Games	PPG	RPG	APG	SPG
2006–2007	POR	57	16.8	4.4	4.0	1.2
2007–2008	POR	74	19.1	4.7	5.8	1.1
2008–2009	POR	78	22.6	4.7	5.1	1.1
CAREER		**209**	**19.8**	**4.6**	**5.1**	**1.1**

(PPG = points per game; RPG = rebounds per game;
APG = assists per game; SPG = steals per game)

achievements

All-Star selection: 2008, 2009
Rookie of the Year Award: 2007
Pacific-Ten Conference Player of the Year: 2006
NCAA All-American: 2006
Scored game-high 18 points at 2008 All-Star Game

rookie: a first-year player

fact | On January 24, 2009, Roy had 10 steals in one game. His effort set a Portland record.

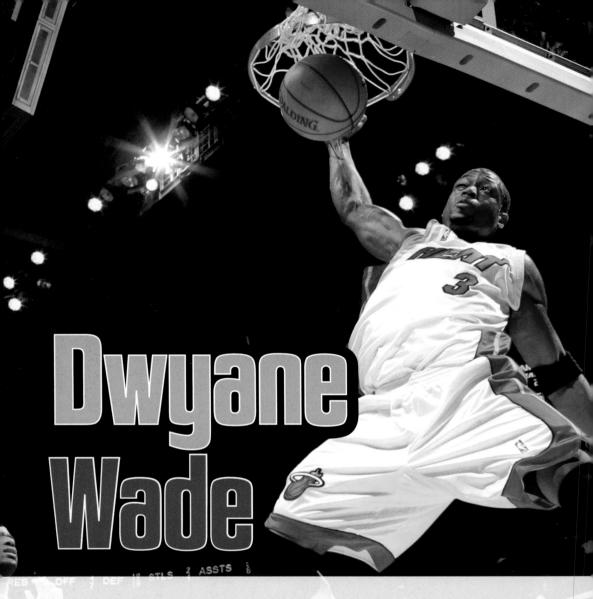

Dwyane Wade

One of Dwyane Wade's nicknames is "Flash." It's no secret why. Wade is lightning-quick with the basketball. He can beat almost any defender off the **dribble**. He can also slash to the basket or pass to an open teammate. In the 2006 NBA Finals, Wade averaged 34.7 points per game while leading the Miami Heat to the championship.

Name: Dwyane Tyrone Wade
Born: January 17, 1982, in Chicago, Illinois
College: Marquette University
Height: 6 feet, 4 inches
Weight: 216 pounds
Position: Guard

Regular Season Stats

Year	Team	Games	PPG	RPG	APG	SPG
2003–2004	MIA	61	16.2	4.0	4.5	1.4
2004–2005	MIA	77	24.1	5.2	6.8	1.6
2005–2006	MIA	75	27.2	5.7	6.7	1.9
2006–2007	MIA	51	27.4	4.7	7.5	2.1
2007–2008	MIA	51	24.6	4.2	6.9	1.7
2008–2009	MIA	79	30.2	5.0	7.5	2.2
CAREER		**394**	**25.2**	**4.9**	**6.7**	**1.8**

(PPG = points per game; RPG = rebounds per game;
APG = assists per game; SPG = steals per game)

achievements

All-Star selection: 2005, 2006, 2007, 2008, 2009
NBA champion: 2006
NBA Finals MVP: 2006
All-NBA Second Team: 2005, 2006
Member of U.S. Olympic gold medal team: 2008

bounce
the floor

fact | In 2003, Wade led the Marquette Golden Eagles
to the NCAA's Final Four. He was named a
First-Team All-America for his performance.

Glossary

assist (uh-SIST) — a pass that leads to a score by a teammate

block (BLOK) — a defensive play made by swatting away a shot as it leaves an opponent's hands

clutch (KLUHCH) — an important or crucial moment in a game

draft (DRAFT) — the process of choosing an athlete to join a sports organization or team

dribble (DRI-buhl) — to bounce a basketball off the floor

dunk (DUHNK) — when a player jumps up and jams the ball hard through the net

layup (LAY-uhp) — a shot where the ball is gently played off the backboard with one hand and into the basket

paint (PAYNT) — the area directly below and in front of the basket that is painted a different color than the rest of the basketball court

rebound (REE-bound) — to take possession of the ball after it bounces off the backboard or rim

rookie (RUK-ee) — a first-year player

steal (STEEL) — to take the ball away from an opposing player

Read More

Doeden, Matt. *The Greatest Basketball Records*. Sports Records. Mankato, Minn.: Capstone Press, 2009.

Smithwick, John. *Meet LeBron James: Basketball's King James*. All-Star Players. New York: PowerKids Press, 2007.

Stewart, Mark. *Swish: The Quest for Basketball's Perfect Shot*. Minneapolis: Millbrook Press, 2009.

Internet Sites

FactHound offers a safe, fun way to find Internet sites related to this book. All of the sites on FactHound have been researched by our staff.

Here's all you do:

Visit *www.facthound.com*

FactHound will fetch the best sites for you!

Index